MW01136269

ISBN: 978-1-7383041-3-4
Printed in USA
First Edition

To Splinter and Spike

A Note for Parents and Guardians

We believe that learning about money can be one of the greatest adventures. Our mission is to make this journey as fun and inspiring as possible, empowering your kids to make wise, confident financial choices.

How to use this book:

- **Solve Together:** Each chapter starts with a fun mystery revealing a money concept. Read the stories and solve puzzles along the way!
- **Pick Your Path:** Each chapter is a standalone mini-adventure, so jump in wherever your child is interested!
- **Money Chats:** Use quirky questions and trivia to spark lively discussions about money and plan your family's next adventure!
- **Real-World Practice:** Help your child apply what they've learned—whether it's managing allowance, setting savings goals, or budgeting for family fun!

Thanks for bringing "Money Adventures" into your home. Here's to raising the next generation of savvy spenders and brilliant budgeters!

A Note for the Young Adventurers

We're here to show you that money isn't just grown-up stuff—it's everywhere, from the tooth fairy to the video games you love. And the more you know about it, the more you can do with it!

Inside Your Adventure Book:

- **Mysteries to Solve:** Each chapter opens with a thrilling mystery about money—like the "Adventure of the Lost Wallet." Can you solve it and uncover the secrets of smart spending?
- **Color as You Learn:** Make this book truly yours by adding a splash of your favorite colors to the cool illustrations inside!
- **Exciting Money Games:** The fun challenges and games inside might just spark your very first business idea. How cool would that be?
- **Cool Money Trivia:** Did you know that there are ATMs in Antarctica or that the first coins were used over 2,500 years ago? This book is packed with amazing trivia that shows how exciting money can be!

Learning about money now is like planting a seed that will grow into your future successes. Who knows? The next great idea for a business or invention might come right from these pages!

Get ready, set up your crayon box, and dive into "Money Adventures".

Enjoy the Ride!

Table of contents

Chapter 1

Introduction to Money

Story Time:
"The Secret of the Ancient Coin"

History of Money

Did you Know?

Would You Rather?

Design your own Currency

"The Secret of the Ancient Coin"

Part 1
A mysterious discovery

In the heart of Rivertown, Emma, Jake, and Zoe were exploring the old creek when they found a strange, heavy coin covered in unfamiliar symbols.

"Look at this!" Emma said, holding up the coin. "Do you think it's worth something?"

Curious, they visited Mr. Thompson, the town historian. He examined the coin and said, "This might be from a time before money as we know it. Back then, people used a barter system." To explain, Mr. Thompson gave them a riddle:

"I am used for trade, but I'm not money's face,
Just goods exchanged in a different place.
A basket for a pail, without coins or bills,
What am I? Solve this with your skills!"

Emma, Jake, and Zoe quickly answered, "The barter system!"
"Exactly," Mr. Thompson said. "This coin might be an early attempt to make trade easier."

"The Secret of the Ancient Coin"

Part 2
Possible Possibilities

Inspired, the kids embarked on a mission to trace the coin's origins. Their next stop was the local library. They sifted through old maps and records that hinted the coin was minted right in Rivertown, possibly as part of a forgotten local currency.

The librarian gave them another riddle to solve:

"I'm old and faded, my past a mystery,
I might be found in a dusty history.
To find me, look where old records lie,
What am I? Give it a try!"

After some thought, the kids answered, "Historical records!"

The librarian pointed them to a collection of old maps that might lead to more clues.

"The Secret of the Ancient Coin"

Part 3
Clues from the past

Their investigation led them to Mrs. Lee, an elderly collector of ancient currencies. She revealed that the coin was rumored to be part of a treasure hidden by the town's founders. The treasure was meant to teach future generations about the importance of money in creating economic stability.

Mrs. Lee presented them with a riddle:

"Hidden from view, yet shining bright,
A place where history takes flight.
Find me near the old and wise,
Where the past and present harmonize."

The kids guessed, "Near historical landmarks!"
Mrs. Lee nodded and handed them an old map that marked key landmarks around town.

"The Secret of the Ancient Coin"

Part 4
The Treasure Hunt

With the map in hand, the trio set off on a thrilling treasure hunt. Each landmark revealed a puzzle about the town's history and the evolution of trade and currency.

At the old mill, they found a stone with an inscription:

"Here, laws are written but not with a pen.
I stand tall and silent, guarding the town's men.
I'm built from brick, yet I house what is fair.
What am I?"

The kids answered, "The town hall!"

Deciphering clues led them inside the town hall, where they uncovered ancient logs and decoded messages about the town's economic past.

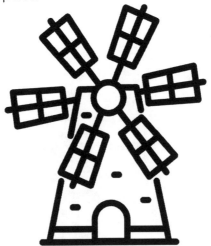

"The Secret of the Ancient Coin"

Part 5
The ending

Their final destination was under the giant oak in Rivertown's oldest park. Digging beneath its roots, they unearthed a hidden chest. Inside were various types of ancient coins and a journal detailing the town's economic history.

Emma read from the journal, "This treasure was meant to show how money, starting from simple coins, revolutionized trade and helped our community prosper."

The kids proudly donated their find to the local museum, celebrating their discovery and the knowledge they gained. They realized that money, beyond just coins and bills, was a tool that helped people reach agreements and build a thriving community.

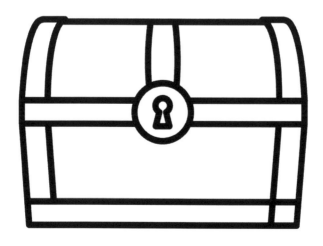

The History of Money

Money has evolved significantly over the ages, transforming from basic barter systems to the complex currency networks we know today.

- **Barter System** (Pre-3000 BCE): Early humans exchanged goods and services directly.

- **First Coins** (Around 600 BCE): The Lydians were one of the first to use coins, making transactions easier.

- **Paper Money** (7th Century): First developed in China during the Tang Dynasty, paper money became a convenient means of transaction.

- **Gold Standard** (1870s-1930s): Many global currencies were pegged to gold, stabilizing international exchange rates.

- **Digital Money** (Late 20th Century): Credit cards and electronic banking reduced the need for cash.

- **Cryptocurrency** (2009): With the creation of Bitcoin, digital currency began operating independently of any central authority.

Did you Know?

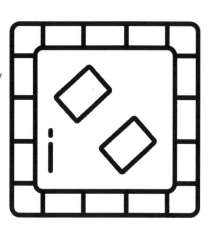

There's more Monopoly money printed in a year than real money printed around the world!

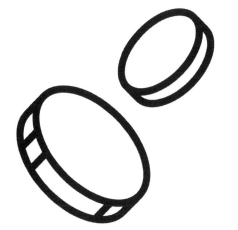

Coins can last in circulation for about 30 years, whereas paper money typically lasts only a few years.

It costs more than one cent to manufacture a single penny.

Did you Know?

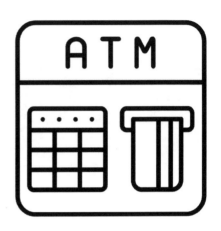

The first ATM was installed in London in 1967, and now there are millions worldwide.

Canada's currency is sometimes called the "loonie" and "toonie" for one and two dollar coins respectively, but another fun aspect is its vibrant colors. The bills are very colorful and even feature transparent windows, making them both pretty and practical!

Currency misprints can be highly valuable, often sought after by collectors.

Would you Rather?

Would you rather be a detective solving the mystery of a missing prized trophy in a haunted school or be the treasurer managing the funds of a secret adventure club?

● ● ● ● ● ● ● ● ● ●

Would you rather find a hidden treasure chest filled with old coins from around the world or find a modern-day treasure chest that contains an unlimited supply of your favorite candy?

● ● ● ● ● ● ● ● ● ●

Would you rather go on a time-travel adventure to barter goods in an ancient market or take a futuristic trip to a space station to use digital currency?

Would you Rather?

Would you rather design your own secret currency that only you and your friends can use, or find a secret map that leads to a hidden vault of gold bars?

● ● ● ● ● ● ● ● ● ●

Would you rather have the ability to double any amount of money you touch once a day or find a rare historical coin once a month that could be worth thousands?

● ● ● ● ● ● ● ● ● ●

Would you rather travel back in time to mint the very first coin ever used, or be in the modern day to design a new digital currency that becomes the most popular in the world?

Design Your Own Currency

- **Choose Your Denominations:** Decide what denominations you will have (e.g., 1, 5, 10, 20).

- **Design the Layout:** Use paper and colored pencils or a digital design tool to create your currency. Include different sizes or colors for different values.

- **Add Security Features:** Design special marks that are only visible under UV light or intricate patterns that are hard to replicate.

- **Cultural Symbols:** Incorporate symbols that represent your culture or imaginary society.

- **Name Your Currency:** Give your currency a unique name that reflects the values or history of the society it belongs to.

Create your design on the next page and share your designs with friends or family, and discuss what makes your currency unique and trustworthy!

Design Your Own Currency

Chapter 2

Earning Money

Story Time:
"The Case of the Business Riddles"

Did you Know?

Would You Rather?

Tips for starting a Business

Business ideas for Kids

Plan your Mini-Business

"The Case of the Business Riddles"

Part 1
The Big Idea

Lily, Max, and Zoe were excited about summer vacation and wanted to earn some extra money for a new adventure park they had heard about.

They brainstormed creative ideas and decided to start a "Neighborhood Fun Fair" in their backyard.
As they planned, Lily presented a riddle to her friends:

"I'm a way to earn some cash,
From lemonade stands to art you splash.
A fair where you can play and win,
What's the name of this fun-filled spin?"

Max quickly answered, "A fun fair!"
The kids got to work, setting up booths for games, crafts, and snacks, determined to make their fair a hit.

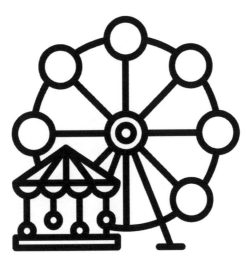

"The Case of the Business Riddles"

Part 2
The Crafty Challenge

The day of the fair arrived, and the backyard was bustling with excitement. Zoe had set up a craft booth where kids could make their own friendship bracelets. To make it more fun, she created a riddle for each customer:

"I'm a loop of colors, bright and neat,
To show you care, I'm quite a treat.
Wear me on your wrist or give to a friend,
What am I that you can make and mend?"

One child guessed, "A friendship bracelet!"

Zoe smiled and let them pick out their own beads and charms, making each bracelet a special creation.

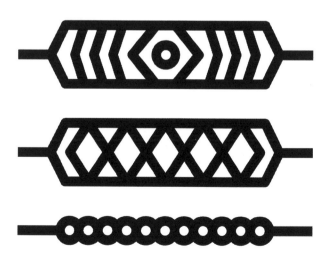

"The Case of the Business Riddles"

Part 3
The Game Booth Mystery

Max ran a game booth where kids could win small prizes by completing fun challenges. To add an extra twist, he included a riddle for each game:

"I'm a circle with a spinning spin,
Hit me right and prizes you'll win.
At the fair, I make things fun,
What am I that spins for everyone?"

Lily guessed, "A spinning wheel!"

The spinning wheel game became a favorite, and the kids enjoyed playing while winning small toys and treats.

"The Case of the Business Riddles"

Part 4
The Snack Attack

Lily's snack booth was the most popular, with homemade cookies and lemonade drawing in crowds. To make things interesting, she set up a riddle competition:

"I'm cold and sweet, a drink for the day,
With lemons and ice, I chase thirst away.
What am I, the drink you crave,
On a hot summer day, cool and brave?"

A customer answered, "Lemonade!"

The snack booth was a huge success, with everyone enjoying Lily's delicious treats.

"The Case of the Business Riddles"

Part 5
The Final Surprise

By the end of the day, Lily, Max, and Zoe were thrilled with their earnings and the positive feedback from their neighbors. They had earned enough money for their adventure park visit and had a blast doing it.

Before wrapping up, they gathered their friends for one last riddle:

"We worked together and had some fun,
Now it's time to see what we've won.
With creativity and teamwork so grand,
What did we earn from our fair, hand in hand?"

Their friends shouted, "Money for the adventure park!"

The kids celebrated their successful fair and planned their next adventure, proud of their hard work and creativity.

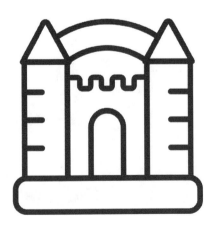

Did you Know?

In 2014, a 15-year-old named Kenneth Shinozuka invented a device to assist patients with Alzheimer's disease, showing how kids can impact serious fields like healthcare.

Some pets earn millions! Grumpy Cat, for example, earned more than $100 million from appearances and merchandise.

Ryan Kaji of Ryan's World was once the highest-earning YouTube star, generating over $22 million in a year from toy reviews, all starting when he was just three years old.

Did you Know?

With technology becoming more ingrained in everyday life, tech-savvy kids can offer their skills to teach older adults how to use smartphones, computers, or social media platforms.

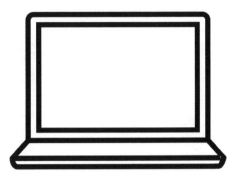

Dorothy Straight became the youngest published author when her book was published in 1964 at the age of four.

In the 1800s, children as young as six were often employed in factories and mines due to their ability to fit into small spaces that adults couldn't.

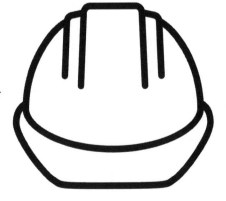

Would you Rather?

Would you rather start a summer business that is super busy but for only one month or a less busy one that goes all summer?

• • • • • • • • • •

Would you rather earn money by doing a unique one-time job that pays a lot or a regular job that pays small amounts over time?

• • • • • • • • • •

Would you rather save all your earnings for one big purchase or spend a little along the way on smaller treats?

Would you Rather?

Would you rather work with friends in a team to earn money or start your own independent business?

● ● ● ● ● ● ● ● ● ●

Would you rather make money by organizing fun events for your friends, like a mini-carnival or movie night, or by doing individual tasks like tutoring or crafting?

● ● ● ● ● ● ● ● ● ●

Would you rather start a business that involves working outdoors, like gardening or car washing, or a business that you can run from inside your home, like a baking or jewelry-making business?

Tips for Starting a Business

Business Ideas for Kids

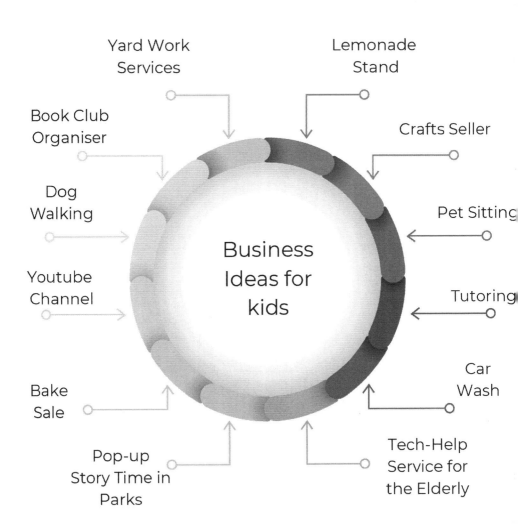

Yard Work Services

Lemonade Stand

Book Club Organiser

Crafts Seller

Dog Walking

Pet Sitting

Youtube Channel

Business Ideas for kids

Tutoring

Bake Sale

Car Wash

Pop-up Story Time in Parks

Tech-Help Service for the Elderly

Plan your Mini-Business

Objective: *Create a business plan for a mini-business you can start in your neighborhood.*

Instructions:

- **Business Idea:** Choose what kind of business you want to start (e.g., lemonade stand, dog walking, craft sales).

- **Materials Needed:** List all the materials you'll need to start and run your business.

- **Pricing Strategy:** Decide how much you will charge for your goods or services.

- **Marketing Plan:** Think about how you will tell people about your business. Will you make flyers, use social media, or tell friends and family?

- **Financial Goals:** Set a goal for how much money you want to make. Then, plan how much of that money you will save, spend, and possibly donate.

- **Operation Plan:** Decide when and where your business will operate. What days of the week? What hours? What locations?

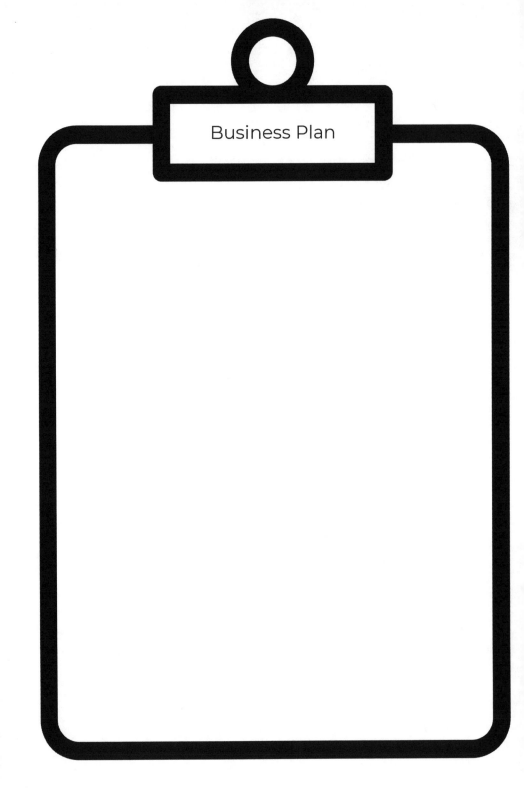

Business Plan

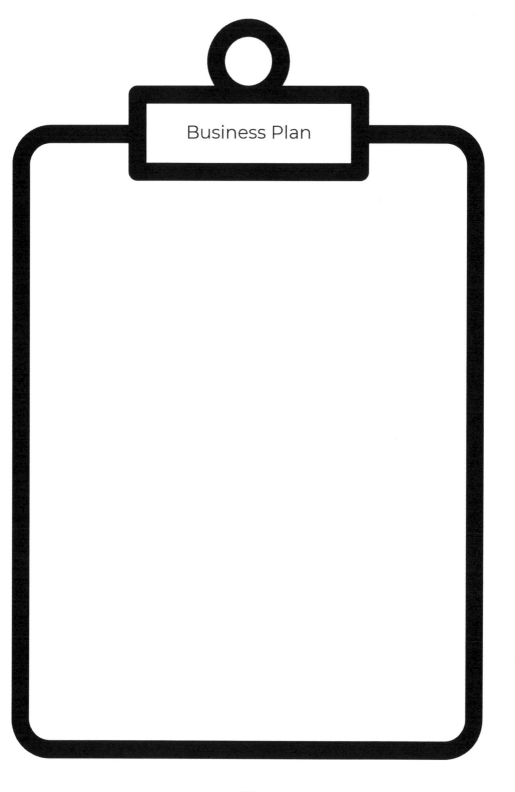

Business Plan

Business Plan

Chapter 3

Saving Money

Story Time:
"The Magical Silver Piggy Bank"

History of Saving Money

Impact of Saving Money

Did you Know?

Would You Rather?

Modern Money Saving Tools

Design your own Savings Chart

More Savings Activities

"The Magical Silver Piggy Bank"

Part 1
The Mysterious Gift

Max and Mia, a brother and sister duo, woke up to a rainy Saturday morning to find a curious package on their doorstep.

Wrapped in shiny silver paper was a piggy bank shaped like a spaceship, gleaming under the droplets.

Attached to it was a cryptic note, written in bold letters: "Fill me up to unlock a treasure beyond your wildest dreams."

The kids were instantly captivated, wondering who sent it and what treasure it could possibly hold. They made a pact to save every penny they could find, determined to uncover the mystery.

"The Magical Silver Piggy Bank"

Part 2
The First Clue

After weeks of saving their allowances, and even starting a small lemonade stand, the piggy bank finally showed signs of change.

One evening, as they counted the coins to see their progress, the piggy bank began to glow faintly. Surprised, Max shook it slightly, and a small, rolled-up piece of paper fell out.

It was a clue! The clue led them to the oldest tree in their backyard, where, after some digging, they uncovered a rusty old key with the initials "S.B." and the number "50" engraved on it.

The mystery deepened, and their curiosity grew.

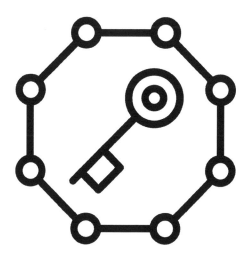

"The Magical Silver Piggy Bank"

Part 3
The Puzzle Pieces

Max and Mia realized that the key and the number might indicate that more clues would come as they continued to save.

Energized by their find, they devised new ways to earn money—from selling old toys online to helping neighbors with small tasks.

Every time their savings reached another 50 coins, the piggy bank glowed again, revealing a new clue.

Each clue took them on a mini-adventure: to the local library's hidden archives, behind the park's waterfall, and even inside the spooky attic of the old Henderson house.

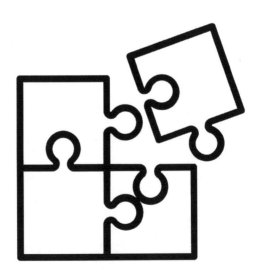

"The Magical Silver Piggy Bank"

Part 4
The Secret Vault

With each adventure, they pieced together the history of their town and the legend of a forgotten treasure hidden by the town's founder, Silas Blackburn.

The final clue led them back to the community center where a large portrait of Silas hung. Using the rusty key, they discovered a hidden compartment behind the painting.

Inside was a small vault with a digital keypad. Recalling the number "50," they entered it, and the vault clicked open, revealing an assortment of old, valuable coins and a dusty ledger filled with names, including their great-grandparents'.

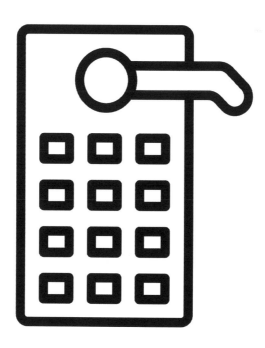

"The Magical Silver Piggy Bank"

Part 5
The Treasure Revealed

The ledger detailed how the town's residents had contributed to a community fund during tough times, which helped everyone thrive.

Each name was a person who had saved and helped others, preserving the spirit of community and support. Inspired, Max and Mia decided to continue the legacy.

They used some of the coins to fund a community project and planned to teach their friends about saving and helping others.

As they walked home, their piggy bank glowed warmly, as if approving of their decision to carry on the tradition of kindness and community support.

History of Saving Money

Ancient Egypt and the Grain Banks

In ancient Egypt, people grew a lot of grain, but they didn't eat it all right away. They saved it in huge buildings called granaries. This was very smart because if there wasn't enough rain one year and the crops didn't grow, they still had plenty of grain saved up to eat.

Medieval Tontines

In the Middle Ages, a financial instrument called a tontine was popular, particularly in France and Italy. Participants would contribute to a common fund, and as members passed away, their shares would be redistributed among the surviving members. This arrangement encouraged saving and provided support for older members of the society as their numbers dwindled.

Roman Clubs for Saving

In Ancient Rome, people had clubs where everyone put in a little bit of money. This way, if someone got sick or needed help, the club could use the money everyone saved to help out. It was like having a big group of friends who all promised to look out for each other.

The Impact of Saving Money

- **Keeping Money Safe and Growing:**

A long time ago in Egypt, people stored extra grain to use when food was scarce, like during a famine or war. In Athens, they kept reserve funds for similar reasons.

- **Helping Each Other Out:**

 In ancient Rome, there were savings clubs where people helped each other with money during tough times. In medieval times, there were groups called tontines that did something similar.

- **Creating New Ways to Use Money:**

A long time ago in China, people started using promissory notes, which are like saying "I owe you" on paper. This idea helped start other money practices like writing checks and using paper money today.

- **Old Ideas, New Uses:**

The way people stored grain in Egypt a long time ago is similar to how countries today keep oil in case there's a shortage. Also, the idea of helping each other with money in ancient Rome is like how we have insurance and pensions now to help us when we're older or if something unexpected happens.

Did you Know?

Earlier, people had to smash the piggy bank to get to their coins. This was a way to make sure that the money was saved until it was really needed.

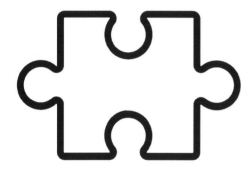

In Japan, there's a traditional type of piggy bank called an "Ichimatsu," which is designed to encourage saving. You have to solve a small puzzle to open it, making saving money both fun and challenging

The world's largest piggy bank was created in 2015 and measured over 14 feet long and 8 feet tall! It was made by the Shikoku Bank in Japan to teach children about saving money.

Did you Know?

The oldest known savings account book belonged to and a Dutch girl named Elisabeth Brachthuizer from the 18th century. Even 300 years ago, people were tracking their savings!

Today, some digital savings accounts are set up to help you save your spare change automatically. When you buy something, these accounts round up your purchase to the nearest dollar and put the difference into savings!

Studies have shown that having savings can actually make you healthier. People with savings generally have less stress and better health outcomes, partly because they worry less about financial emergencies.

Would you Rather?

Would you rather save up for one big toy you've wanted all year, or spend your money right away on lots of little toys?

● ● ● ● ● ● ● ● ● ●

Would you rather have a piggy bank that doubles your money in a year, or a magic wallet that gives you a dollar every day you don't spend any money?

● ● ● ● ● ● ● ● ● ●

Would you rather do a job you really enjoy for a small amount of money or a job you don't like for lots of money?

Would you Rather?

Would you rather have a chance to win a $50 toy in a contest or get a guaranteed $10 now to save?

• • • • • • • • • •

Would you rather give up buying snacks for a month to buy a new video game, or keep buying snacks and save slower for the game?

• • • • • • • • • •

Would you rather lend your money to a friend who needs it for a school project or keep it in your savings for something you want?

Modern Money Saving Tools

Savings Accounts: It's like a magic chest that adds more coins the longer you keep your money inside!

Retirement Accounts: Save and watch your money grow for a grand adventure when you're older.

Treasury Securities: Lend your money to the government, and get more back later

Education and Health Savings Accounts: Save and grow your money for cool school stuff or health.

Robo-Advisors: Robot friends who are smart with money, helping your money grow in the best spots.

Savings Apps: These apps are like a mini wizard in your pocket, helping you save and spend wisely.

Design your own Savings Chart

What You'll Need:
- Colorful paper or a poster board
- Bright markers or crayons
- Cool stickers
- A ruler
- A pencil

Steps to Create Your Chart:
- Pick Your Goal: Think of something awesome you want to buy, like a toy or a game. Make sure you know the price. Eg. $50.
- Draw Your Chart:
  - Use the ruler and pencil to draw a big rectangle with several small boxes inside from left to right.
- Label Your Chart:
  - Write your saving goal (the price) at the top.
  - Mark each box with a number, starting from $1 up to how much you need to total the price.
  - eg. If you want tp save $50 you could have 25 boxes in your chart of $2 each.
- Decorate:
  - Color your chart and make it fun!
  - Add stickers in each box when you save! Be creative!
- Track & Celebrate:
  - When all boxes are full, do a happy dance—time to buy your dream item!

Savings Activities

DIY Piggy Bank:
Activity: Make your own piggy banks using recycled materials like old jars, boxes, or bottles.
How It Works: Decorate the containers with paint, stickers, or glitter.

Family Savings Challenge:
Activity: Initiate a family challenge where everyone works together to save towards a common goal, like a family outing or a new board game.
How It Works: Each family member contributes regularly to the family savings pot. Track progress together and celebrate when the goal is reached.

Save the Change:
Activity: Teach kids to save their change after purchases.
How It Works: Whenever they buy something, any change received goes directly into their savings. Over time, even small amounts of change can add up to a significant sum.

Chapter 4

Spending Money

Story Time:
"The Needs vs Wants Quest"

Needs Vs Wants

Budgeting Explained

Did you Know?

Would You Rather?

Budget Balloon Pop

"The Needs vs Wants Quest"

Part 1
The Mysterious Invite

In Willowville, best friends Max, Lily, and Sam found a golden envelope under the school's old oak tree. Addressed to "The Clever Minds of Willowville," it contained an invitation from Mr. Cedric Green:

"Dear Brave Souls,

Embark on a thrilling quest at Green Manor to unravel the Mystery of Needs and Wants. This adventure will test your wisdom and courage, with a grand prize for those who succeed.

Yours respectfully, Mr. Cedric Green"

Excited and slightly apprehensive, the trio set off on their bicycles towards Green Manor, their hearts full of anticipation for the adventure ahead.

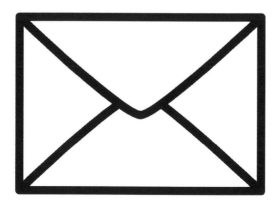

"The Needs vs Wants Quest"

Part 2
The Challenge Begins

Upon reaching Green Manor, the trio was welcomed by Mr. Green, a lively elder with twinkling eyes.

"Welcome, young adventurers! Your first task is in the grand library," he said, guiding them through hallways lined with portraits.

The library was immense, filled with towering bookshelves. Their task was to categorize scattered items—books, a compass, designer clothes, a camping stove—into needs, essential for life, and wants, which are not essential but provide comfort.

While sorting, Sam discovered a curious leather-bound book titled Economics with a hidden note inside:

"Beyond the daily bread,
where stories are fed,
the first key lies ahead."

Intrigued, they realised this was referring to the library, "Where stories are fed" and kept the note for further clues.

"The Needs vs Wants Quest"

Part 3
Puzzle in the Pantry

Mr. Green's next challenge brought them to a large, rustic pantry. "Prepare a meal using only essential ingredients," he instructed. "This will teach you about the basic needs for a healthy life."

The pantry was stocked with an array of foods from rice to eggs. The friends chose rice, beans, vegetables, and fruit, discussing how each item was important for nutrition.

Lily, reaching for a bag of rice, found it oddly heavy.

Behind it was a hidden latch that opened to reveal a dusty, narrow staircase. "We'll explore this after dinner," whispered Max, excited by the prospect of uncovering more secrets.

"The Needs vs Wants Quest"

Part 4
The Secret Staircase

That night, armed with a flashlight and a sense of adventure, they crept into the pantry and down the stairs.

The staircase led them to an underground chamber, a hidden room filled with luxurious items—video games, expensive sneakers, and the latest electronics. A plaque on the wall read:

"Wants can bring joy, but needs keep us alive."

At the room's end, another note awaited them:

"I hold the secrets of wealth and trade,
Where choices are made and prices are weighed.
Look for me where knowledge flows,
In pages that reveal how money grows."

They realized this clue and the one they had found earlier pointed them back to the library—to the economics book they had seen earlier.

"The Needs vs Wants Quest"

Part 5
The True Treasure

Back in the library, they solved the riddle by pulling out a book titled "Economics." This triggered a clicking sound; a section of the wall swung open to reveal a cozy, hidden study filled with books on financial literacy and wise decision-making.

Mr. Green appeared, clapping delightedly. "Congratulations! You've learned that understanding your needs and managing your wants wisely is key to a stable and happy life."

He awarded each child a small savings bond, promising them it was the seed to grow their future wisely.

Biking home under starlit skies, the friends cherished their adventure—not just for the fun, but for the valuable insights they gained to navigate life's choices.

Needs Vs Wants

Needs: These are things you must have to live and be healthy. They are the super important stuff! Eg. Food to eat, a place to live, clothes to
wear, and going to the doctor when you're sick.

Wants: These are things that are fun to have but you won't be in trouble without them. They are like the bonus levels in a game!
Eg. Toys, video games, candy, or a fancy bike.

Why It's a Big Win to Know This:

More Adventures Await: If you save well, you can have more money later for a super cool adventure—like a trip to an amusement park or getting that awesome new video game console when it comes out.

Be the Captain of Your Ship: By choosing wisely between wants and needs, you get to be the boss of your money. It's like being the captain of a ship and steering it wherever you want to go!

"Money is like a toolbox—it's not just for spending, but for building your dreams!"

So managing your money between needs and wants is also called Budgeting. Let's find out what that is.

Budgeting Explained

Let's explore how budgeting helps you handle your money like a pro!

What is Budgeting?
Imagine you have a treasure map. Instead of leading you to buried gold, this map shows you how to spend your money wisely!

Count Your Coins
Start by figuring out how much money you have. This could be from your allowance, a gift, or money you earned from doing chores.

Plan Your Shopping Adventure
Think about what you need to buy. Needs are things like school supplies or a new pair of shoes. Wants are fun things like toys or games!

Draw Your Map
Create a plan on paper. Write down your needs and wants and how much each thing costs. Make sure you don't spend more money than you have!

Set Aside Some Treasure
Always keep some money aside for later. This could be for something big you want in the future, like a bicycle or a video game console.

Budgeting Explained

Follow Your Map

Use your plan when you spend money. This helps you buy what you need and still have money left for fun stuff and saving!

Review and Update Your Map

Sometimes, you might spend more or less than you planned. That's okay! Check your map often and change it if you need to. This keeps your spending on track!

Budgeting is like being the captain of your own ship. You decide where your money goes, and make sure you have enough for both fun treasures and necessary supplies!

Did you Know?

If you save just 50 cents a day in a jar, by the end of the year, you'll have over $180!

Buying video games that are a year old instead of the newest releases can save you more than half the price. More games, less money!

Every book or movie you borrow from the library is money saved. If each book costs $15 and you read 20 books a year from the library, that's $300 saved!

Did you Know?

If you drink water from a
reusable bottle instead of
buying a bottle every day for $1,
you can save about $365 in a
year.

Using coupons for groceries or
activities can cut costs
significantly. Some families save
hundreds of dollars a year just
by using coupons!

Did you know that shopping
during sales can save a lot of
money? For example, if you buy a
toy that's normally $20 during a
50% off sale, you only spend $10.
That's like getting two toys for
the price of one!

Would you Rather?

Would you rather save up for one big toy you've wanted all year or buy small toys every month?

• • • • • • • • • •

Would you rather save $1 every day for a whole year to buy something big, or have $30 to spend right now on whatever you want?

• • • • • • • • • •

Would you rather use your allowance to buy snacks every day after school or save it to buy a cool new outfit for your birthday?

Would you Rather?

Would you rather have a big party once a year or small parties throughout the year?

● ● ● ● ● ● ● ● ● ●

Would you rather go to a matinee movie with all your friends or a prime-time show just with your best friend?

● ● ● ● ● ● ● ● ● ●

Would you rather borrow video games from the library or own them but have fewer games overall?

"Budget Balloon Pop Game: Needs vs. Wants"

- **Budget**: Each player start with $100.

- **Pop and Place:** Colour in a balloon to 'pop' it. Write the item and its cost under "Needs" or "Wants".

- **Discuss:** Explain why you categorized each item. If all players agree then place it in the right category. eg. Books can be essential for knowledge or just a "want". Discuss and decide.

- **Budget Tracking**: Subtract each item's cost from your budget. Record remaining budget after each purchase.

- **Budget Management:** Players must manage their tokens wisely. Running out of budget ends the game for that player.

- **Total Up:** Calculate your spending in each category. Note any leftover funds.

- **Scoring:** Each "Need" is 10 points. Each "Want" is 7 points. Player with most points wins.

"Budget Balloon Pop Game: Needs vs. Wants"

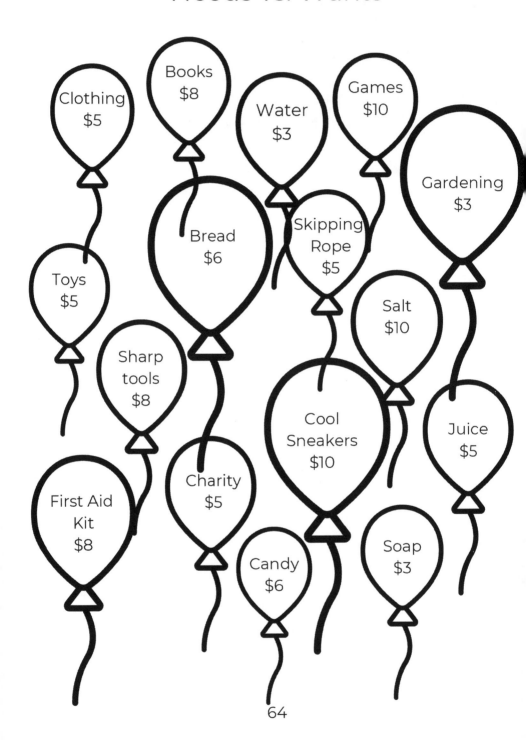

Clothing $5

Books $8

Water $3

Games $10

Gardening $3

Toys $5

Bread $6

Skipping Rope $5

Salt $10

Sharp tools $8

Cool Sneakers $10

Juice $5

First Aid Kit $8

Charity $5

Candy $6

Soap $3

Player Name:			Player Name:		
Budget	"Need'"	"Want"	Budget	"Need'"	"Want"
Total $	Total Points		Total $	Total Points	

Chapter 5

Banking Basics

Story Time:
"The Hidden Vault"

History of Banking

Meet the Banking Team

Did you Know?

Would You Rather?

Design your own Cool Bank

"The Hidden Vault"

Part 1
The Vault and the First Riddle

Jenna, Max, and Leo couldn't believe their luck when they found themselves spending the summer at Grandpa's old house. The best part? The ancient vault in the basement, which hadn't been opened for years.

One afternoon, while exploring the basement, Leo spotted a dusty ledger next to the vault. Inside was a note:

To those who are clever, this riddle I leave,
Solve it correctly, the treasure you'll retrieve.
What has branches, but no leaves, trunk, or bark?

Suddenly, Grandpa appeared, chuckling. "You've stumbled upon one of the old banking riddles! Solve it if you can, but beware—solving one leads to another."

Jenna thought for a moment. "A bank!" she exclaimed.
Grandpa nodded. "That's right! But the real adventure is just beginning."

The kids' excitement grew as Grandpa handed Max a brass key. "This key opens the first lock, but there are two more, each with a riddle."

Max inserted the key, and the first lock clicked open. Another riddle appeared:

"The Hidden Vault"

Part 2
The Second Lock

They gathered around the vault as the second riddle lit up on the panel:

I can be deposited or withdrawn,
But I'm not something you can hold.
I grow with time and patience. What am I?

Leo scratched his head. "Something that can be deposited or withdrawn... but not held?" he muttered.

Jenna's face lit up. "It's interest! You deposit money in a bank, and interest grows over time!"

Grandpa smiled, and with a click, the second lock opened. "There's still one more lock to go," Grandpa said. "Get ready!"

"The Hidden Vault"

Part 3
The Final Lock

The kids eagerly awaited the next riddle, which appeared as the vault door clicked again:

What has a face but no heart,
Moves money quickly, that's just the start?

Max grinned, "It's a credit card! You can use it to move money without handling cash."

"Very good!" Grandpa said, as the final lock clicked open. The heavy vault door slowly creaked open, revealing a small metal box sitting on an old wooden desk.

"There's one more challenge," Grandpa said, pointing to the combination lock on the box.

"The Hidden Vault"

Part 4
The Final Challenge

The note on the box read:

To open this box, the answer you seek,
Is found in a riddle, clever and sleek.
I'm the number of days it takes for most checks to clear,
Multiply by two, and the code will appear.

Jenna thought for a moment. "How long does it take for checks to clear?"

"Usually about three days," Max said. "So, three times two is six."

They tried entering 006 into the combination lock.

With a click, the box opened! Inside, they found old banknotes, a faded photo of young Grandpa standing in front of a bank, and another note.

"The Hidden Vault"

Part 5
The Treasure

The note read:

You've found the treasure,
but there's more to explore.
Follow the map to where the old tree grows.

Leo grabbed the map, and the kids rushed to the oak tree. After digging, Max found a small chest with another note:
What is full of money but never makes a sound?

"An ATM!" Jenna shouted, opening the chest to reveal a small golden key.

Grandpa smiled. "Well done! This key opens something special."
In his study, Grandpa unlocked a drawer and read a letter:

Dear Jenna, Max, and Leo,
This adventure is just the start. The real treasure is the knowledge you gain along the way. You're now Bankers of Imagination. More mysteries await!"

History of Banking

- **Barter Trades:** Before money, people swapped items like toys for chickens—very tricky!
- **Gold and Silver Coins:** People started using shiny coins, which were easier to carry but attracted pirates and thieves.
- **Safe Temples:** The first banks were temples in ancient Greece and Rome, where coins were kept safe because temples were well-guarded.
- **Medieval Money Benches:** In medieval Italy, money lenders worked from benches ("bancas") in markets. If a lender ran out of money, his bench was broken—this is where "bankrupt" comes from.
- **Modern Banks:** Today, banks do a lot! They keep money safe, help buy houses, start businesses, and more. They even move money around the world using computers and the internet.
- **Pocket Banks:** Nowadays, you can even have a bank in your pocket with digital banking on smartphones!

Meet the Banking Team

Meet some of the superheroes who keep our banks running smoothly.

The Friendly Bank Teller:
- Superpower: Speed and Accuracy!
- Role: Helps people with deposits and withdrawals and ensures every penny is perfect.

The Clever Loan Officer:
- Superpower: Making Dreams Come True!
- Role: Helps people get money for big things like houses and schools.

The Detective Fraud Investigator:
- Superpower: Super Sleuthing Skills!
- Role: Keeps an eye out for bad guys trying to steal money.

The Genius IT Specialist:
- Superpower: Tech Wizardry!
- Role: Makes sure all the bank's computers and apps work perfectly.

The Master Bank Manager:
- Superpower: Leadership!
- Role: Looks after the whole bank and solves any big problems.

Did you Know?

The largest bank vault in the world can hold over $100 billion —that's like a mountain of money!

Brink's trucks, which move money from banks, are built to be as tough as tanks!

There's enough money in the world to stack bills to the moon and back—twice!

Did you Know?

The Federal Reserve Bank of New York holds the world's biggest gold vault, deep beneath the streets!

The door of the largest bank vault in the world weighs about the same as two elephants!

The world's first paper money was created in China about 1,200 years ago, and people thought it was like magic because it was so light and easy to carry!

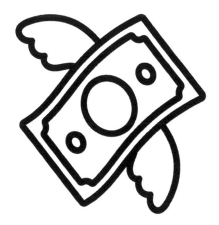

Would you Rather?

Would you rather have a piggy bank that oinks every time you save a coin or a silent one that glows in the dark?

● ● ● ● ● ● ● ● ● ●

Would you rather be the manager of a bank where all the customers are animals or one where all the customers are superheroes?

● ● ● ● ● ● ● ● ● ●

Would you rather visit a bank made entirely of LEGO bricks or a bank that's built like a giant treehouse?

Would you Rather?

Would you rather design a new coin with your face on it or design a new paper bill with your favorite animal on it?

• • • • • • • • • •

Would you rather keep all your savings in a treasure chest buried in your backyard or safe in a bank under the sea?

• • • • • • • • • •

Would you rather go on a tour of the oldest bank in the world or spend a day learning secret handshakes from a bank security team?

Design Your Own Cool Bank

What You Need:
- Pencils or crayons

Let's Get Creative!
- **Name your Bank:** Give it a cool name!
- **Sketch your bank!** Add a place for the tellers, an ATM spot, and a cool play area!
- **Decide What Your Bank Does:** List the cool things your bank offers, like saving up for games or quick cash for toys!
- **Make It Safe:** On the second sheet, think of awesome ways to keep your bank safe—like spy cameras or even a superhero guard!
- **Create a Fun Logo:** Draw a catchy logo and some fun ads that show why your bank is the best!
- **Present It:** Show off your bank to friends or family and explain what makes it super special.

Have a blast building your dream bank!

Chapter 6

Investing

Story Time:
The Great Investment Quest

Investment Tools

Investment Tools Explained

Did you Know?

Would You Rather?

Activity: Investing Puppet Show

"The Great Investment Quest"

Part 1
The Puzzle of the Golden Ticket

In the heart of Wonderville, three friends—Ella, Tom, and Ava —found a sparkling golden ticket in a box of old toys. The ticket had a message:

"To find the treasure that's hidden from view,
solve the puzzles and learn what investments do.
Stocks, bonds, and funds are your clues;
follow them well to discover the news."

Eager to start their adventure, the friends set off to solve the first puzzle.

"The Great Investment Quest"

Part 2
The Stock Adventure

Their first clue led them to the local playground, where a giant slide was decorated with images of different companies. A friendly clown named Mr. Shares gave them a riddle:

"I'm like a piece of a company's dream.
Invest in me, and your money may gleam.
Find the company on the slide that's shining bright,
and the next clue will be in your sight."

Ella, Tom, and Ava found the company "Sunny Pops" on the slide and received the next clue:

"Now go to the place where people lend their cash. Look for a sign with a bond in a flash."

"The Great Investment Quest"

Part 3
The Bond Balloon Hunt

They followed the clue to a balloon artist at a street fair. Each balloon had a note about bonds—how they let people lend money and get it back later. They popped balloons to find the next clue hidden inside:

"To move ahead, go to where the investments are shared. It's a place where money is pooled and cared."

"The Great Investment Quest"

Part 4
The Mutual Fund Treasure Hunt

The clue led them to a giant sandbox with different sections labeled "Stocks," "Bonds," and "Funds."

They had to dig in the "Funds" section to find a hidden key. Each section had fun facts about how mutual funds work, like how they pool money from many investors to buy a variety of assets.

They found the key and received the final clue:

"To find the treasure, think
where kids like to explore,
a place full of stories
and knowledge galore."

"The Great Investment Quest"

Part 5
The Discovery

They went to the local library and searched through the children's section. Behind a bookshelf, they found a small chest with their golden ticket. Inside the chest was a letter:

"Congratulations! You've completed the Great Investment Quest. The true treasure is the knowledge you've gained and the fun you've had learning about investing."

Ella, Tom, and Ava were thrilled with their adventure and celebrated their newfound understanding of investments!

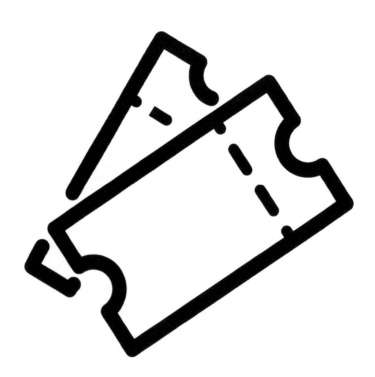

Investing Tools

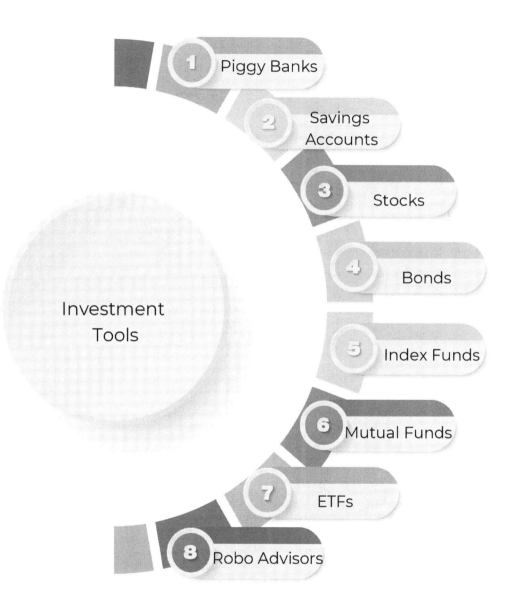

Investment Tools

1. Piggy Banks
2. Savings Accounts
3. Stocks
4. Bonds
5. Index Funds
6. Mutual Funds
7. ETFs
8. Robo Advisors

These are all explained in more detail in the following pages

Investing Tools Explained

Piggy Banks

- What It Is: A small, cute container where you keep your money safe.
- How It Works: When you put money in, it stays there until you need it or decide to use it.
- Fun Fact: Piggy banks help you save up for something special, like a toy or a book!

Savings Accounts

- What It Is: A special place at a bank where you keep your money and earn a tiny bit of extra money over time.
- How It Works: You deposit money into the account, and the bank pays you a little extra for saving.
- Fun Fact: Savings accounts are like having a super-safe piggy bank that also gives you a little reward!

Investing Tools Explained

Stocks

- **What It Is:** Pieces of a company that you can buy, which means you own a small part of that company.
- **How It Works:** If the company does well, your stock can become more valuable, and you might earn money.
- **Fun Fact:** Owning stocks is like having a tiny say in how your favorite toy company is run!

Bonds

- What It Is: A way of lending your money to someone (like the government) for a certain time in exchange for extra money later.
- How It Works: You give them your money, and they promise to pay you back with a bit of extra money.
- Fun Fact: Bonds are like giving a friend a loan and getting a thank-you gift when they pay you back!

Investing Tools Explained

Mutual Funds

- What It Is: A collection of many different stocks and bonds put together in one big "basket."
- How It Works: You invest money into this basket, and it's managed by experts who make decisions for you.
- Fun Fact: It's like having a mixed box of chocolates, where each piece (investment) is different but together they're tasty!

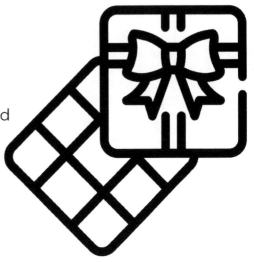

Index Funds

- What It Is: A type of mutual fund that invests in a bunch of companies making up a specific list or "index."
- How It Works: Your money is spread out across many companies in the index, helping reduce risk.
- Fun Fact: Index funds are like a school lunch tray with a little bit of everything – fruits, veggies, and snacks – so you get a balanced meal!

Investing Tools Explained

Exchange-Traded Funds (ETFs)

- What It Is: Similar to index funds but traded like stocks on the stock market.
- How It Works: You buy shares of the ETF, which holds many different investments, and you can trade it anytime.
- Fun Fact: ETFs are like having a toy box with a variety of toys that you can swap with friends whenever you want!

Robo-Advisors

- What It Is: Automated tools that help you invest your money based on your goals and preferences.
- How It Works: You answer some questions, and the robo-advisor uses that info to decide where to invest your money.
- Fun Fact: Robo-advisors are like having a super-smart robot friend who helps you pick the best investments!

Did you Know?

The Dutch East India Company, founded in 1602, was the first company ever to sell shares to the public. It's like being part of the world's first big adventure club!

The New York Stock Exchange (NYSE) is the world's largest stock market. It has thousands of companies listed, like having a giant treasure chest with many different treasures inside!

In 1961, NASA's first spaceflight cost $80 million. Today, private companies are investing in space travel, and it's expected to be a $1 trillion industry by 2040. Investing in space is like being part of a galactic adventure!

Did you Know?

The stock market sometimes gets compared to a candy store because there are so many choices! Picking stocks is like choosing your favorite candies from a giant sweet shop.

$$\frac{72}{\text{Rate of Return}} = \text{Time for Investment to Double}$$

There's a trick called the "Rule of 72" that helps you estimate how long it will take for your money to double. Just divide 72 by your investment's annual return rate. It's like a magical formula !

The 20% rule in investing says you should aim to save and invest at least 20% of your money. It's like setting aside a special treasure chest for future adventures!

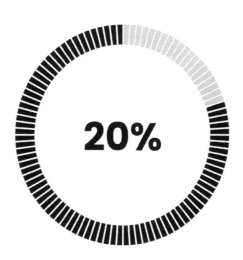

20%

Would you Rather?

Would you rather invest in a company that makes awesome toys or a company that builds cool video games?

● ● ● ● ● ● ● ● ● ●

Would you rather own a share in a space travel company or a share in a company that makes super cool robots?

● ● ● ● ● ● ● ● ● ●

Would you rather invest in a company that creates fantastic new books or one that designs amazing amusement parks?

Would you Rather?

Would you rather have a map that shows where to find hidden investment treasures or a robot that helps you decide where to invest your money?

● ● ● ● ● ● ● ● ● ●

Would you rather have a magic notebook that writes down the best investment ideas or a special savings account that earns you extra money just for saving?

● ● ● ● ● ● ● ● ● ●

Would you rather invest in a company that makes delicious candy or one that creates amazing new gadgets?

Investment Puppet Show

What You Need:
- Puppet-making materials (socks, paper bags, markers, etc.)
- Puppet scripts or scenario cards

How to Play
- **Create Puppets**: Use simple materials to make puppets representing different investments (e.g., a "Stock" puppet, a "Bond" puppet, etc.).
- **Write Scripts:** Provide short scripts or scenarios where the puppets explain their type of investment and the pros and cons of that investment.
  Use information given in this chapter to help write the script.
- **Perform:** Use the puppets to act out investment scenarios and teach each other about investing.
- **Vote:** Have family members/audience vote for any one investment puppet based on the script and the puppet with the most points wins!

Investment Puppet Show
Script Example

Stocky the Stock:
(Excitedly)
"Want quick growth? Choose me, Stocky!"
Bondy the Bond:
(Nods)
"For steady returns, Bondy's your choice!"
Savings Sam:
(Smiling)
"Need safety? Savings Sam is here!"
Mutual Fund Marty:
(Spreads arms wide)
"For a mix of fun and safety, try Mutual Fund Marty!"
Narrator:
(Off-stage voice)
"Which investment will you pick? Each one has its own perks! Thanks for visiting Investment Land!"

Chapter 7

Debit & Credit

Story Time:
"The Case of the Missing Dollars"

History of Debit and Credit

Real-world examples of Debit and Credit

Why are Credit Cards called Credit Cards?

Why Understand Debit and Credit?

Did you Know?

Would You Rather?

Activity: Debit Credit Sorting Race

"The Case of the Missing Dollars"

Part 1
The Missing Money

One day, Mia and her little brother, Jake, were counting their allowance. Every week, their parents gave them a small amount of money for helping with chores. But today, something was wrong.

"Mia, I think we're missing some money!" Jake exclaimed as he looked at his empty piggy bank.

Mia frowned. "You're right. We had more last week. Where did it go?"

Just then, they noticed a mysterious note on their table. It read:

If your money seems to disappear,
look where debits and credits are near.

"What does that mean?" Jake asked.

"I'm not sure," Mia said. "But I think we need to figure it out!"

"The Case of the Missing Dollars"

Part 2
The Detective's Ledger

Mia decided they should play detective. They got a notebook and drew two columns, labeling one "Debit" and the other "Credit."

"Mom and Dad told us that when we spend money, it's called a debit, and when we get money, it's called a credit," Mia explained.

Jake added, "So, if we spent our allowance, it would be a debit. And when we got our allowance, it was a credit!"

They wrote down everything they could remember about spending and getting money. But something was still missing.

"The Case of the Missing Dollars"

Part 3
The Riddle of the Balance

As they puzzled over the ledger, another note appeared. This one had a riddle:

To find what's lost, you must balance the scales,
Where debits and credits tell their tales.

Mia thought hard. "I think this means our debits and credits should add up. If we spent too much or forgot to add something, the balance will be off."

They checked their ledger and realized they forgot to write down the money Jake spent on a toy last week. Once they added it, the numbers made sense.
"Our money didn't disappear—it just got spent!" Jake said, relieved.

"The Case of the Missing Dollars"

Part 4
The Magic of Double Entry

Just when they thought the mystery was solved, their dog, Max, knocked over a box of coins. As Mia and Jake picked them up, they noticed some coins were missing. Another note floated down:

One entry's fine, but two are better,
To keep your money safe forever.

Mia realized, "This must be about double entry. When we write down a debit, we should also write down the credit. That way, we always know where our money is."

They added the missing toy to both sides of the ledger—debit for spending, credit for getting the toy. Suddenly, the lost coins reappeared!

"The Case of the Missing Dollars"

Part 5
The Final Puzzle

With their ledger balanced, Mia and Jake thought they were done. But the final note appeared, with one last challenge:

To finish the case and end your quest,
Balance the numbers to pass the test.

They carefully checked their ledger one last time, making sure every debit had a matching credit. When they were sure everything was correct, the note changed to a message of congratulations:

"You've solved the case! Remember to always keep track of your debits and credits, and your money will never vanish again."

Mia and Jake high-fived, proud of their detective work. They had learned an important lesson about keeping track of their money, and they were excited to tell their parents all about it.

History of Debit and Credit

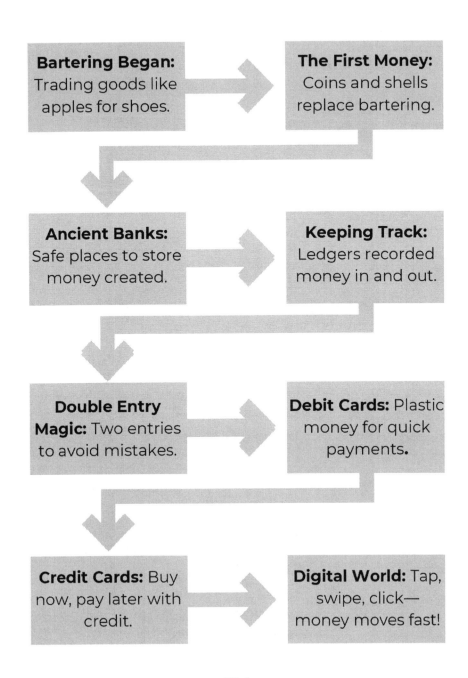

Bartering Began: Trading goods like apples for shoes.

The First Money: Coins and shells replace bartering.

Ancient Banks: Safe places to store money created.

Keeping Track: Ledgers recorded money in and out.

Double Entry Magic: Two entries to avoid mistakes.

Debit Cards: Plastic money for quick payments.

Credit Cards: Buy now, pay later with credit.

Digital World: Tap, swipe, click—money moves fast!

Real-world Examples of Debit & Credit

Real World Examples of Debit

- Buying Ice Cream: You use your allowance to buy an ice cream cone. The money is taken out of your bank account—that's a debit.

- Video Game Purchase: You save up and buy a new video game. The money leaves your account—another debit.

- School Lunch: You swipe your lunch card at school to buy lunch, and the money is taken from your account —that's a debit.

Real World Examples of Credit

- Birthday Money: You receive $20 from your grandparents for your birthday. It goes into your account—that's a credit.

- Allowance Day: Your parents give you your weekly allowance, and it's added to your account—that's a credit.

- Prize Money: You win a contest at school and get a prize of $10. This money gets added to your account— that's a credit.

Why are Credit Cards called "Credit" Cards?

In banking, credit means money that is added to your account. It can be money you receive, like when someone pays you, when you deposit cash into your bank account, or when you earn interest from the bank.

When you see a credit on your bank statement, it means your balance has gone **up**—more money has been added to your account.

Credit can also mean the ability to **borrow** money from the bank or a lender, like with a credit card. In this case, credit refers to the money the bank lets you borrow with the promise that you'll pay it back later.

So even though you're spending, it's the bank's money at first, so it's called a "credit" card.

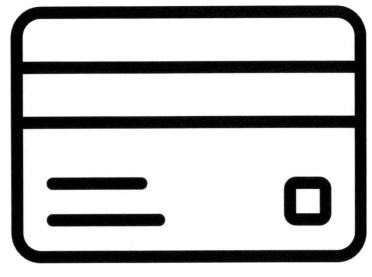

Why Understand Debit and Credit

Protect Your Money: Know where your coins go so you don't run out.

Spend Smartly: Save up for cool things you really want.

Become a Money Hero: Use your skills to reach your goals and have fun!

Grow Your Savings: Watch your money grow with allowances and gifts.

Avoid Surprises: Always know how much money you have.

Understanding debit and credit is like having superpowers that help you manage your money wisely and achieve awesome things!

Did you Know?

The very first credit card was called the "Diners Club Card" and was used in 1950 to pay for meals at restaurants!

Some debit cards are as small as a keychain! They're called "mini cards" and are super handy.

Debit card transactions are lightning fast—most take less than 5 seconds to process!

Did you Know?

Grown-ups have something called a "credit score" that works like a high score in a game. The better they manage their credit, the higher their score!

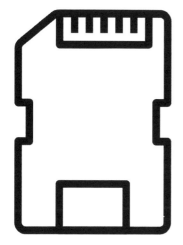

Some debit cards have a special chip that keeps your money extra safe, kind of like a shield in a video game!

Did you know you can design your own debit card with your favorite characters or colors? Some banks let you create custom cards!

Would you Rather?

Would you rather always use a debit card that gives you a cool sound effect every time you spend money, or a credit card that lets you choose a new card design every month?

• • • • • • • • • •

Would you rather get a bonus credit every time you do your homework, or a bonus debit every time you help with chores?

• • • • • • • • • •

Would you rather keep track of your debits and credits by writing them down in a special adventure journal, or by using a fun app that turns it into a game?

Would you Rather?

Would you rather earn credits by solving fun riddles, or by completing exciting challenges like treasure hunts?

• • • • • • • • • •

Would you rather have a debit card that gives you a surprise gift once a month, or a credit card that lets you earn double points for every dollar you spend?

• • • • • • • • • •

Would you rather get a debit card that gives you instant cash back on everything you buy, or a credit card that lets you save up for a huge reward at the end of the year?

Debit and Credit Sorting Race"

What You Need:
- Two containers or baskets labeled "Debit" and "Credit" for each player
- Small pieces of paper with simple transactions written on them (e.g., "Bought candy," "Got birthday money")

How to Play:
- Start the Race: Spread out the transaction cards on a table or floor.
- Sort the Cards: Players race to pick up the cards and drop them into the correct container (Debit or Credit) as fast as they can.
- Check the Sorting: After the race, go through the containers to see who got the most correct.
- If playing alone, set a timer and beat your own time!

Chapter 8

The Digital World of Money

Story Time:
"The Case of the Virtual Wallet"

Digital Money Types and Tools

How Online Transactions Work

Digital Money Safety Tips

Cryptocurrency

Did you Know?

Would You Rather?

Design your own Digital Coin

"The case of the Virtual Wallet"

Part 1
The Digital Dilemma

Oliver, Emma, and Max, the best friends known for solving mysteries, got a call from Mr. Stevens, their tech-savvy neighbor. "Someone broke into my virtual vault and stole my digital coins!" he exclaimed.

The kids knew this was no ordinary mystery. Mr. Stevens was known for his high-tech gadgets and secure digital vaults. How could someone possibly break in?

The kids rushed over and saw a strange riddle on his computer screen:

"I hide in plain sight, invisible to the eye,
When you need me, just say the word, and I'll come by.
What am I?"

"The case of the Virtual Wallet"

Part 2
The Hidden Password

The kids gathered around their clubhouse to figure out the riddle. Max, the tech expert, thought hard. "Invisible to the eye... It must be something digital," he muttered.

Emma snapped her fingers. "What if it's the password? It hides in plain sight, but you can't see it unless you know what it is!"

"Exactly!" Oliver said. "We need to figure out Mr. Stevens' password to see if it was stolen."

But just as they cracked the first riddle, another appeared on their clubhouse wall, projected from a hidden device:

"I'm always on the go but never leave my spot,
I have hands that move, though running I'm not.
I count every second, hour, and day,
What am I, ticking away?"

"The case of the Virtual Wallet"

Part 3
The Race Against Time

The kids rushed to solve the new riddle. "It's a clock!" Emma said excitedly. "The hands keep time, but the clock itself doesn't move!"

"Yes, but what does a clock have to do with digital money?" Max wondered aloud.

They hurried back to Mr. Stevens' house, where they found an old-fashioned clock on his desk. Behind the clock was a USB drive.

"Maybe the key to the vault is on this drive!" Oliver said. But when they plugged it in, a message appeared: "Access denied."
Frustrated, they noticed another riddle on the USB drive:

"I am the key to everything,
Without me, you'll get nothing.
I open doors, but I'm not a key.
What am I?"

"The case of the Virtual Wallet"

Part 4
The Digital Key

"Could it be a code?" Max suggested. "Digital money and vaults always use codes!" Emma nodded. "But what kind of code opens everything?"

They pondered for a moment before Oliver exclaimed, "It's a PIN number! Without the right PIN, you can't access anything."

The kids quickly returned to Mr. Stevens' computer and tried different PIN combinations. Finally, they entered a sequence that matched the riddle's clues.

With a beep, the computer screen flashed, and the digital vault opened, revealing a list of recent transactions. But something was off—there were transactions that Mr. Stevens hadn't made!

Another riddle popped up on the screen:
"I travel the world without leaving home,
I carry your treasures wherever you roam.
What am I?"

"The case of the Virtual Wallet"

Part 5
The Discovery

The kids huddled together to solve the last riddle. "It sounds like a digital wallet!" Emma said. "It stores digital money and you can use it anywhere without moving."

They traced the transactions to an online store, where they discovered someone had been using Mr. Stevens' digital wallet to buy expensive gadgets.

With a quick call to the store's customer service, the kids helped Mr. Stevens track down the thief—a notorious hacker who had been stealing digital money all over town.

Thanks to the kids' sharp minds and quick thinking, the hacker was caught, and Mr. Stevens' digital coins were returned. As a reward, Mr. Stevens taught the kids all about online safety and how to protect their digital money.

Digital Money Types and Tools

 Online Bank Accounts: A digital piggy bank you can use anytime.

 Digital Wallets: A magical wallet on your phone for easy payments.

 Gift Cards: Digital tickets to buy stuff at your favorite stores.

 Mobile Payment Apps: Pay by waving your phone, no cash needed.

 Cryptocurrency: Online-only money, like a secret digital treasure.

 Virtual Coins in Games: Earn or buy coins to unlock cool game rewards.

 Online Allowance Apps: Get your allowance digitally and manage it online.

How do online Transactions Work?

Picture your digital piggy bank full of coins, ready to go.

Spot that awesome toy or game you've been eyeing online.

Add to cart and hit the "Pay Now" or "Checkout" button.

Type in your info, like your email and payment method.

Your bank gets a message to send your money to the seller.

Your bank checks your balance and zips the money over to the seller.

You'll get a receipt that says, "You've paid!" and your item is on the way.

Your money lands safely with the seller, and your new treasure is coming soon!

Digital Money Safety Tips

Strong Passwords:
Create a tough-to-crack password.

Two-Factor Authentication:
Add an extra security step.

Avoid Sharing:
Keep your passwords secret.

Beware of Phishing: Don't fall for
tricky emails or messages.

Use Secure Websites:
Look for the lock symbol when
shopping online.

Monitor Your Account:
Regularly check your
account for sneaky activity.

Update Software: Always use
the latest version of your
apps.

Cryptocurrency : How it all began

Cryptocurrency started in 2008 with a mystery! Someone using the name Satoshi Nakamoto had the idea to create a new kind of money that only exists online.

This became the first cryptocurrency, called Bitcoin. In 2009, the first Bitcoins were created, and people began using them, even buying pizza with them!

As Bitcoin became more popular, other digital coins, like Ethereum and Litecoin, were created, each with their own special features. By 2017, cryptocurrency was so popular that everyone wanted to join the adventure.

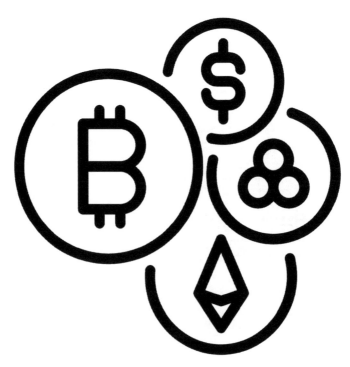

Cryptocurrency : How it Works

The Magical Internet Treasure

Cryptocurrency is like a special treasure you find only on the internet. It's money that lives inside your computer or phone, not in your piggy bank!

Digital Coins

Cryptocurrency is like magical digital coins. You can use them to buy things online, just like real money, but you can only see and use them on your devices!

Your Secret Treasure Chest

To keep your digital coins safe, you need a special treasure chest called a digital wallet. This wallet is like a super-secret safe that only you can open with your own special password.

Cryptocurrency : How it Works

The Hidden Map
Whenever you use your digital coins, it's recorded on a hidden map called the blockchain. This map keeps your coins safe and makes sure no one can steal them.

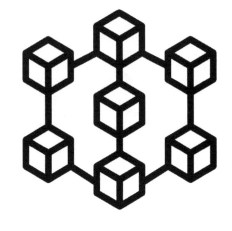

Earning New Coins
Some people use powerful computers to solve puzzles and earn new digital coins. This is called mining—like digging for treasure, but with computers!

Using Your Treasure
You can use cryptocurrency to buy things online, trade it, or save it for later. It's like having your own treasure chest ready whenever you need it.

Did you Know?

Credit card company Visa, can handle over 65,000 transactions in one second—that's faster than a blink!

In 2010, you could buy 1 Bitcoin for less than a dollar. Today, 1 Bitcoin can be worth tens of thousands of dollars—

Cryptocurrency is super secure because of something called the blockchain. It's like a giant, unbreakable lock that keeps your digital money safe.

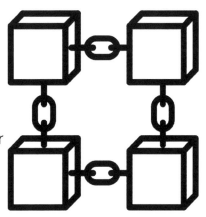

Did you Know?

Did you know someone once bought two pizzas with 10,000 Bitcoins? Today, those Bitcoins would be worth millions of dollars—making it the most expensive pizza ever!

In some countries, people use their mobile phones as their primary bank! Services like M-Pesa allow users to send, receive, and save money using only text messages.

In Sweden, over 80% of all payments are made digitally. Some stores there don't even accept cash anymore—it's all digital!

Would you Rather?

Would you rather pay for everything with a tap of your phone or by smiling at a camera?

• • • • • • • • • •

Would you rather earn digital coins by playing your favorite video game or by solving fun puzzles online?

• • • • • • • • • •

Would you rather pay for all your school snacks using a QR code or by using a cool wristband that scans like magic?

Would you Rather?

Would you rather shop at a store where everything is bought with virtual coins or at a store where you pay by answering fun riddles?

● ● ● ● ● ● ● ● ● ●

Would you rather receive all your birthday money as digital gift cards or as a code you can redeem for your favorite online games?

● ● ● ● ● ● ● ● ● ●

Would you rather use digital money to buy real-world toys delivered to your door or to unlock special items in your favorite online game?

Design your own Digital Coin

What You Need:
- Paper
- Markers, crayons, or colored pencils
- Craft supplies (stickers, glitter, etc.)
- Scissors

Steps:
1. Name and Draw Your Coin:
   - Think of a fun name like "StarCoin" or "RainbowCoin."
2. Choose Features:
   - Decide on special features (e.g., changes color, gives bonuses).
   - Write down the special features of your coin.
   - Eg. Adventure Boost: Can only be spent on fun adventures or Kindness Bonus: Gives you half back when used to help others.
3. Share Your Design:
   - Show your coin and explain what makes it unique.
4. Display It:
   - Hang your coin up to show off your work.

The End

"Money, like a tool, can help you build great things, but it's how you use it that counts."
– Unknown

Hope you enjoyed the book!

Stay tuned for the
next book in this series!

Made in the USA
Middletown, DE
13 October 2024